Cathy,

May you al
follow your heart
desire.

♡ Jenny

"*Embracing Your Life,* is filled with beautiful quotations, each inspiring on its own, each energizing and awakening. The author shows discernment and an inclusive spirit. A book to refer to frequently for the poetic beauty and the delightful images. The synthetic effect of the poetry of those who are in touch with greater light and love, and who speak as the soul, the true Self, has a unique power to lift and aid others.

— LaUna Huffines, author of *Healing Yourself with Light: How to Connect with the Angelic Healers* and *Bridge of Light: Tools of Light for Spiritual Transformation*

"Insightful, wise, and visually charming, *Embracing Your Life* serves up a stimulating dose of inspiration, spiritual fuel and a gentle nudge to awaken the divine and unique love we all carry within us. A lovely book and true gift from the heart."

— Julie Moriva, *songwriter*

"Simple yet profound, Jenny Vainisi's advice comes straight from her heart. *Embracing Your Life* is a gem of a book and useful for connecting more deeply to all areas of your life."

— Mary Beth Sammons, author of *Living Life as a Thank You* and *Second Acts that Change Lives*

"What a lovely book! The illustrations are so beautiful, as are the choices of written material. It is a book to keep close by."

— Jody Uttal, author/painter of *Painted Prayers*

Embracing Your Life

Embracing Your Life

A Guide for Living With Gratitude and Appreciation

Jenny Vainisi

Embracing Your Life
A Guide for Living With Gratitude and Appreciation

For further information contact:

Vainisi Design Studio
58 Middagh Street
Brooklyn, NY 11201
info@embracingyourlifebook.com
www.embracingyourlifebook.com

Publisher's Cataloging-in-Publication
(Provided by Quality Books, Inc.)

Vainisi, Jenny.
   Embracing your life : a guide for living with gratitude and appreciation / Jenny Vainisi.
      p. cm.

   LCCN 2011938061
   ISBN-13: 978-0-615-56526-2
   ISBN-10: 0615565263

   1. Self-acceptance. 2. Gratitude.   I. Title.

BF575.S37V35 2012   158.1
                                       QBI11-600180

Printed in USA

This book is lovingly dedicated to my parents who taught me the many ways of embracing my life. You mean everything to me.

And to my brother —just for being you.

Contents

Introduction

Have you ever discovered a piece of writing at the exact moment when you needed it most? Whose message made you feel as if it had been written especially for you? I certainly have. In fact, the quotes and references gathered in this book are from precious moments of grace when I have felt just like that.

I began this project by collecting thought-provoking passages, which deeply touched me over the years. From these wise words, I was inspired to draw imagery that mirrored their simple, yet often profound insights. This fun, creative process started as play, something I did for my own personal enjoyment and relaxation, but it quickly transformed into an extraordinary inner exploration, one which helped me connect to my deepest self through a medium that is most sacred to me — my art.

How do you connect with the inner most part of yourself? Is it through yoga? Meditation? Singing? Curling up with your favorite pet? Conversing with a dear friend? Or simply following the whispers of your

heart to wherever they may lead? *Embracing Your Life* celebrates all of these and more, offering simple tools that I have discovered to help you gently connect with your heart.

Our modern, busy lifestyle constantly bombards us with unrealistic images and notions, suggesting our lives are not what they should be: we don't have enough, are not good enough and haven't met some lofty ideal standard of living. I have personally discovered that when I let go of cultural and self-imposed judgement, and stop trying to be something I am not, there is much more room to become who I was meant to be. And I am deeply grateful for that. *Embracing Your Life*, gently reminds you that all aspects of you and your life are worth celebrating, that the simplest things are often those which make it the most precious and meaningful.

I hope you find these passages and illustrations as inspirational as I do. May they comfort and lift you and touch the joy within. May they serve as a reminder to connect with the wisdom of your heart, and to remember that at our very core we are all expressions of love.

Do not wish to be anything but what you are,
and try to be that perfectly.

—*St. Francis de Sales*

Love

The opening of your heart —
to yourself and to others.
Love is our true essence.

Love is spirit, and all experiences of love, however insignificant they seem, are actually invitations to the cosmic dance. Within every love story hides the wooing of the gods and goddesses.

—*Deepak Chopra*

I want to give thanks . . .
For love, which lets us see others
As God sees them.
—*Jorge Luis Borges*

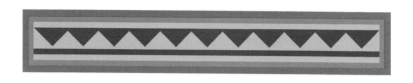

One word frees us of all the weight and pain of life:
That word is love.

—*Sophocles*

Love is the most powerful force in the Universe. We experience our true essence when we abide in its sublime energy. Gazing through the eyes of love, we recognize the Divine in everyone and everything. We expand into our highest wisdom, and achieve our greatest potential. The more intimate we become with our own divinity, the easier it is to extend outwardly, thereby, becoming channels for God's work. In the transcendent state of love, it's clear to see we are all connected. We are all One.

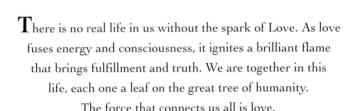

There is no real life in us without the spark of Love. As love
fuses energy and consciousness, it ignites a brilliant flame
that brings fulfillment and truth. We are together in this
life, each one a leaf on the great tree of humanity.
The force that connects us all is love.

—*John Pierrakos*

*I am a Divine being. I honor the love
I have for myself and see it reflected
in the eyes of others. I see
God in human form.*

It is only with the heart that one can see rightly;
what is essential is invisible to the eye.
—*Antoine de Saint-Exupéry*

Even when a river of tears courses through this
body, the flame of love cannot be quenched.
—*Izumi Shikibu*

Perhaps everything terrible is in its deepest being
something that needs our love.
—*Rainer Maria Rilke*

Love is never lost. If not reciprocated, it will flow
back and soften and purify the heart.

— Washington Irving

When life challenges us with a difficult situation, perhaps the best way we can approach it is with love. Bring tenderness to the pain inside your heart, and feel it soften. Search beneath the surface of any conflict. Look behind a person's harsh words. You'll find that hidden within an overly reactive response, lives the truth of what is really transpiring, and being felt.

When we seek to understand deeper meanings, transformation is possible. Setbacks instantly become opportunities for insight and growth. Remember, even masked by defenses, we are all angels deserving of forgiveness, acceptance, and love.

All pain is turned into medicine through love.

—*Rumi*

I am the light of beauty and truth.
I am sweetness and desirability.
I am love. —*Emmanuel*

The whole business of love is to open a window in the
heart, to illumine the breast with the Beauty of the Beloved.
Open a window to God and gaze upon that Face.

—*Rumi*

If we could read the secret history of our enemies, we
should find in each man's life sorrow and suffering
enough to disarm all hostility.

—*Henry Wadsworth Longfellow*

We can do no great things.
Only small things with great love.
—*Mother Teresa*

Everyone has a personal history replete with experiences that have molded us into who we are today. Though each story is distinct with its own painful circumstances, there exists an inherent, common thread in all of them. We all suffer the same wounds of shame, rejection, and abandonment—no matter how they were inflicted. Is it not possible then, to view even our most challenging enemies as kindred beings who hurt just as much as we do? Deep within, we are all lost children longing for love, in need of compassion and care. When we offer these healing gifts to another, we become an integral part in healing the world.

I am gentle and compassionate with myself.
When I hold myself in tenderness
I can be tender with another.

Love attracts love. The love we give out returns to us multiplied. The love that we feel for others is a reflection of the love at the seat of our being. We may think that we love another person because of who they are and what they have done. But, in fact, we love because it is the nature of our being.

—*Susan Santucci*

Be glad of life because it gives you the chance to love and to work and to play and to look up at the stars.

—*Henry van Dyke*

A joyous spirit is evidence of a grateful heart.
— *Maya Angelou*

Gratitude begets gratitude. It's a simple concept, yet we constantly complicate it by comparing ourselves to others, instead of appreciating all that we have at this very moment. Perceiving life through this narrow lens creates an "I'm not good enough" perspective that can cause tremendous disappointment.

Shift your mind-set to one of thankfulness. Appreciation for even the smallest gesture replaces thoughts of lack with those of plenty. Begin to view every-day- moments as blessings: enjoying a warm, soothing cup of tea; sharing a heartfelt conversation with an old friend; receiving joyful affection from your pet; relishing the beauty of your child's smile; absorbing the quiet, stillness of the present moment. The more grateful you are for these simple treasures, the more abundant your life will become. It's that easy.

Create a gratitude list that acknowledges all you are thankful for everyday. You'll be surprised at how much you can include. Joy will begin to flow through you, and from you, when you recognize these love-filled blessings. Watch as your list grows longer, and longer, and longer!

Try a simple gratitude meditation by sitting quietly, taking a few, deep breaths, and connecting with your heart center. Visualize all the people and circumstances that elicit appreciation from you. This is one of the quickest ways to gracefully move into the flow of abundance.

I give thanks for my many blessings.

There is a strange frenzy in my head, of birds flying,
each particle circulating on its own.
Is the one I love everywhere?
—*Rumi*

The way of love is not a subtle argument.
The door there is devastation.
Birds make great sky-circles of their freedom.
How do they learn it?
They fall, and falling, they're given wings.
—*Rumi*

Love is love's reward.
—*John Dryden*

We learn to love like birds learn to fly—slowly, steadily, faltering at times—always guided by an internal force. Watching a baby bird learn to fly can be an anxiety-producing experience. The fledgling starts and stops, barely landing on its mark. But with a few practice flights, the novice transforms into an expert flyer.

Through love, we step into the unknown, take a leap of faith, and surrender to the grandeur of tasting our own delicious vulnerability. Each time we say yes to love we learn how to fly just a little bit better. And just as the tiny-winged bird must trust its instinctual ability to take flight, so too must we trust our heart's intuitive wisdom to take a risk in love.

Only from the heart can you touch the sky.
—*Rumi*

I open my heart to love.

But if you love and must needs have
desires, let these be your desires:
To melt and be like a running brook that
sings its melody to the night.
To know the pain of too much tenderness.
To be wounded by your own understanding
of love; And to bleed willing and joyfully.
                    —*Kahlil Gibran*

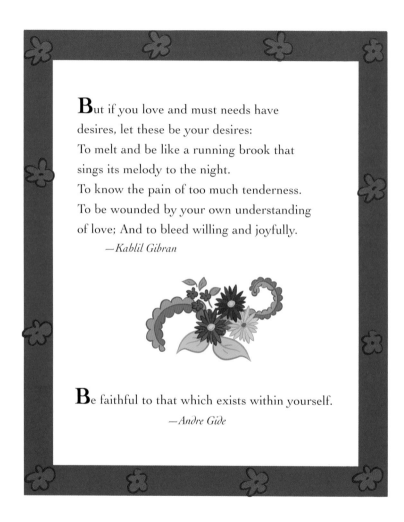

Be faithful to that which exists within yourself.
                    —*Andre Gide*

We here there is love there is life.
—*Mohandas K. Gandhi*

Be faithful to your desires, and to the pull of your heart's longing. Honor the many feelings residing within. Joy, sadness, passion, and grief are just a few that make up an individual's kaleidoscope of emotions. View this expressive multiplicity as your soul revealing itself.

What is flowing in your life? What is out of balance? What needs your attention now? Listen to the gentle whispers emanating from your heart. When we acknowledge and respect what we're feeling in the present moment, we are living in a complete state of truth. Allowing experiences to flow in and pass through, while still remaining connected to our truth, we discover we are exactly where we need to be.

I honor all that I feel, for it is my
souls way of showing
me who I am.

The moment I heard my first love story
I started looking for you—
Not realizing how blind that was
for lovers don't one day find each other
They're in one another all along.

—*Rumi*

Love is, above all, the gift of oneself.
—*Jean Anouilh*

Relationships serve as great teachers by providing opportunities for us to learn and understand. Like a mirror, they reflect back to us what needs attention in life. For example, being consistently drawn to those who are unavailable, or noncommittal, often indicates our inner imbalance projected outward. Ask yourself, "How am I unavailable to *myself*? "Where do I lack commitment in *my life*?" Take a moment right now to notice where in your life you are externalizing a lost, or neglected part of yourself. What can you do to nurture and restore balance?

Conflicts and challenges provide opportunities to better understand our hidden parts, and ultimately release worn out patterns. Like magnets, we attract what needs to be dealt with in our lives. By asking, "What is this experience trying to teach me?" or "What is

the lesson to be learned?" space is created for growth and healing, instead of simply experiencing pain and discomfort.

The love we often search for in another is really our deep longing to re-connect with ourselves. We are drawn to a potential friend or lover with the hope that they will make us whole and complete. Yet no one has the power to complete us more than we do. Our essence is already whole. In Spirit we are complete. In fact, we are perfect.

I learn to love myself more and more.
I share that love with all those
I encounter.

I do not know what it is about you that closes and opens;
only that something in me understands the voice of
your eyes is deeper than all roses.

—*e.e. cummings*

Love is the way messengers from
the mystery tell us things.

—*Rumi*

The river that flows in you also flows in me.

—*Kabir*

Our original nature is love. It is our birthright to express it joyfully, unabashedly, and without conditions. We come into the world so open and innocent, with no fear of love being removed, or used to harm us. Yet as we mature, we begin to close off parts of ourselves. Hurtful experiences, and misconceptions force us to shield our hearts with the intention of protecting it from further wounding. That which once existed as a beautiful, open channel for love becomes choked and constricted.

When we continually guard our hearts, falsely believing this is beneficial, we actually perpetuate the opposite. We shut off love completely, and spend a greater part of our lives trying to compensate for this tragic loss.

But despite our masking efforts, our spiritual essence is, and will always be, love. Just as a rose must emit its inherent, sweet fragrance, so must we express our innate state of love.

Radiating warmth and kindness, I easily give and receive love, allowing my loving nature to joyfully shine. I welcome love, in all it's varied and inspired forms.

No one has yet to fully realize the wealth of
sympathy, kindness and generosity hidden
in the soul of a child.
—*Emma Goldmam*

We see the world clearly when we are children,
and we spend the rest of our lives trying to
remember what we saw.
—*Garrison Keillor*

A child can always teach an adult three things: to be happy
for no reason, to always be busy with something, and to know
how to demand with all his might that which he desires.

—*Paulo Coelho*

Children are sensitive, playful, and curious; they truly experience life with unbridled joy! They remind us of whom we once were, unencumbered by pretense. Perhaps that's why we are drawn to their infectious sense of wonder.

The open, receptive nature of children inspires and refreshes us. It touches our longing to reconnect with the child-spirit within. They set a wonderful example of how we can compassionately tend to this inner child by playing often, seeing the world with new eyes, and most importantly, living in the now.

Recognizing the sacred qualities of children reinforces the importance of nurturing our own inner child. By doing so, we experience the healing warmth of self-love.

Give yourself a gift today by spending time with a child. Notice how your heart fills with joy, and how your mind stays in the present moment. Allow them to guide you back to your basic nature—the essence of love.

> Every adult needs a child to teach;
> it's the way adults learn.
> —*Frank A. Clark*

Have enough courage to trust love one more time.
And always — one more time
—*Maya Angelou*

If only all the hands that reach could touch.
—*Mary A. Loberg*

We sometimes confuse withdrawing, and shielding the heart with being safe, and protective. But love is the opposite of fear, and flourishes when the heart is open, vulnerable, and accessible.

In love's sacred space, we attract more love. In fear's constricted corner, we attract more fear. By trusting love, we enter a courageous state where miracles can happen.

I have found the paradox, that if you love until it hurts,
there can be no more hurt, only more love.

—*Mother Teresa*

I choose to trust love.
My heart is open.

Most of us have appreciated the perfection of the universe,
the animation of living things, the action of the
human mind, and the power of love.

These things all seem to denote a dynamic life force that
surges through everything around us.

This force appears to direct all things, harmoniously,
but irresistibly, towards a natural, definite, useful conclusion.

Is it hard to recognize in this life force a power
greater than ourselves?

— *The Little Red Book*

The closer we come to the center, to the heart of things, the more we find God. If I come to the heart of a human meeting, if I come to the heart of a beautiful woman, if I come to the heart of a dog, I meet God. God's at the heart of everything.
—*Father William McNamara*

Everything responds to the connective energy of love. When the sun bathes a bed of lilies, they reciprocate by sharing their wondrous bloom. When a cat is cradled with sweet tenderness, it responds with purring delight. When we express loving sentiments, we are met with openness and more love!

The Dalai Lama suggests a daily practice for developing loving kindness by connecting with your heart space, and finding the deep well of love and goodness there. Then, while walking down the street, silently send each passing stranger this loving prayer, "I wish you happiness, and causes for happiness." This practice helps you to see through the compassionate eyes of the Divine, and strengthens your loving connection to all beings.

Remember, we are all affecting the world every moment, whether we mean to or not. Our actions and states of mind matter, because we are so deeply interconnected with one another. Working on our own consciousness is the most important thing that we are doing at any moment, and being love is a supreme creative act.

—Ram Dass

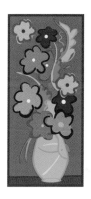

There is little that separates humans from other sentient beings—we all feel pain, we all feel joy, we all deeply crave to be alive and live freely, and we all share this planet together.

—*Mohandas K. Gandhi*

I think I could turn and live with animals, they are so
placid and self-contained. I stand and look
at them long and long.
—*Walt Whitman*

Animals are a healing balm for our mind, body and
soul. If you've had the privilege of sharing your life
with a pet, then you know how deeply these beloved
creatures snuggle their way into your heart. They are
bundles of warm, furry energy that blanket us with
their unconditional love. Even those of the feather-
winged family, or scaly-reptilian variety are capable
of charming their way into our hearts.

The calming and curative effects of animals are widely
recognized. Their presence can influence a variety of
conditions and ailments such as: reducing high blood
pressure, predicting epileptic seizures, and detecting
various cancers. Many work in hospitals as therapy
animals, bringing joy, light, and smiles to patients and
medical workers by simply being there.

Animals unwittingly invite strangers to come together
and chat, often acting as conduits for socialization (as

many dog owners can attest!). Just go to your local dog park and observe how fun and playful the energy can be for both dogs and their owners.

Animals allow those that are shy, and guarded to feel safe enough to reveal their loving nature. In fact, equine therapy offers amazing results when utilized with autistic children, which is capable of transporting them out of their isolated, inner worlds.

They teach us to be nurturing and accepting. They soften us with their soulful gazes, wagging tails, silly antics, and generosity of spirit. Animals make a house a home, and the world a kinder place by the sweet example they set.

Unfortunately, their time spent with us in physical form is limited. But even as they leave us and cross over, our beloved creatures are still teaching us. They demonstrate that in the cycle of life and death, we must eventually let go of all that we love, only to begin again, and again, and again...

Until one has loved an animal, a part of one's
soul remains unawakened.

—*Anatole France*

To the world you may only be one person
but to one person you may be the world.

—*Anon*

My little dog: a heartbeat at my feet.

—*Edith Wharton*

I am holding this cat so it can sleep and
what more is there.
—*Hugh Prather*

Man and animal share a wonderful, and mysterious relationship: a beautiful dance, and exchange of energies that complements both parties.

Animals come to us with so much trust, and unconditional love. Because they ask so little of us, they often receive everything we have to give. They teach us to live spontaneously, and with open hearts. Like shadows, they seemingly become our extended versions

They are always ready to greet us when we come through the door, cuddle and sleep by our side throughout the night, and understand and tolerate all of our moods (even when we are not so pleasant). It is so easy to love a being that is this accepting of us.

Recall the delicious feeling of completeness as a cat rests purring on your lap, or the divine invitation to

open your heart as a dog soulfully gazes into your eyes. A still, peaceful calm permeates the air, resulting in a deeply satisfying connection for both, who feel blessed to be in each other's world.

The smallest feline is a masterpiece.

—*Leonardo Da Vinci*

Spirit

Trusting the divine presence
deep with in you— remeberance
of our highest qualities;
wisdom, power
and love.

In undertaking a spiritual life, what matters is simple:
We must make certain that our path is
connected with our heart.

—*Jack Kornfield*

We must all understand that if we are to be divine,
we must, like the divine, love with divine intensity,
and serve every sentient being on the earth.

—Andrew Harvey

When we come to know our inner God, which is our
true Self, we will know that the divine is in everybody.

—Howard Murphet

The ideas that have lighted my way have been
kindness, beauty and truth.

—Albert Einstein

Spirit lives within you; it lives within your body, in
every cell. You can touch the Great Spirit by
touching your own aliveness.
—*Brooke Medicine Eagle*

What is behind the moon's gravitational pull that
causes the tide to ebb and flow? How do geese intui-
tively know to fly south for winter in V-formation?
Why do seeds and bulbs flourish at exactly the right
time and season?

The entire universe and everything in it is guided and
led by an unseen, internal force. This powerful energy
can also be referred to as Spirit.

We can develop a relationship with Spirit by first
acknowledging it's not an entity outside ourselves. It
is a current within, present in all living creatures and
matter. By recognizing this divine spark in everything,
we begin to see a seamless kinship and connection.

The inherent strength of oak trees reinforces the same attribute in our own being. The delicate grace of bluebells reminds us that we too have a gentle and tender nature. The wild rush of a flowing river taps into our deep longing for freedom.

How blessed are we to be a part of this extraordinary matrix. How blessed are we to realize its power lies within each and every one of us.

Cultivating respect for all life, and recognizing our relationship to it, brings us closer to experiencing the magnitude of Spirit. Our perception of the harsh, external world magically softens as we continually honor this collective, internal pulse.

There is no need for temples; no need for complicated
philosophy. Our own brain, our own heart is our
temple; my philosophy is kindness.

—*His Holiness the Dalai Lama*

Think of yourself as an incandescent power,
illuminated and perhaps forever talked to
by God and his messengers.
—*Brenda Ueland*

Miriam Webster's dictionary defines incandescent as: emitting a visible light; shining brilliantly; to glow. When we are in alignment with our divinity, we are truly lit from within. But how do we personally know when we are "living in the light?"

The radiance of divine nature has many hues. From serene solitude to delirious joy; from peaceful resistance to decisive action; from unconditional self-love to universal compassion. See how many qualities of the divine you can name. Notice how many are shining through you right now.

Learn to allow these innate qualities that are often overlooked or dismissed to emerge and glow. Remember, at our very essence, we are all beings of light and expressions of love.

If we live our beauty we dance with the stars.
—*Deva*

*I am an expression of love and
I am Divine.*

If we open our eyes, if we open our ears, if
we open our hearts, we will find that the
world is a magical place.

—*Chögyam Trungpa*

One can live life as though there are no miracles or
choose to see everything as if it were a miracle.

—*Albert Einstein*

You must have a room, or a certain hour or so a day, where you
don't know what was in the newspapers that morning . . .
a place where you can simply experience and bring
forth what you are and what you might be.
— *Joseph Campbell*

How do you begin your day? Quiet and relaxed, or harried and scrambling? The mode in which you initiate your day can determine the quality of your spiritual connection. Try taking a few minutes in the morning to ease into your life rather than barreling into it. Notice how different this simple adjustment makes you feel.

Prayer and meditation are two significant practices that can assist in connecting to the higher Self. Andrew Harvey describes the delicate subtlety of these two practices. "It has been said that prayer is talking to God (from the heart), while meditation is listening to God (heart to heart)."

Breath is life! Enjoy the peace and stillness that comes from giving yourself a few minutes to meditate in the morning. Focus your awareness on your inhala-

tions and exhalations. Feel your body relax. Relish the potential of a new day. What will it bring? What will you offer? Remembering who you truly are in these tranquil moments will help you remain centered throughout the day.

Try reading a few, reflective lines from an inspirational book. The heart-opening passages will infuse your being with uplifting energy. It's like filling your own, personal vessel with positive reserves that can be utilized throughout the day, especially if you encounter negativity.

Writing in your journal at the beginning of the day helps move you into the beauty of the present moment. Put down thoughts and feelings in an effort to clear your mind and create space. Try writing a prayer, or even a letter to the Divine. Notice the synchronicity that results in response to your heartfelt notation.

Experiencing quiet, reflective time at the beginning of your day, no matter how you create it, brings a rootedness that connects you to Spirit. This, in turn, is what you will radiate to the world.

Divine light and divine love are flowing
through me and radiating from me to
everything around me.

—*Shakti Gawain*

*It may be said that God cannot be known in the
mind only experienced in the heart.*
—*Stephen Levine*

The Tibetan Loving Kindness (Metta) Meditation is a
wonderful and simple way to connect with your heart.
It cultivates feelings of love, happiness, and goodwill
for yourself and others. As you gradually widen your
personal, meditative sphere, you begin to spread lov-
ing kindness to all sentient beings.

Practice the meditation for yourself first, and then
toward others. When you are filled with love and
kindness for yourself, you will overflow, and have
much to give others.

1. Find a quiet spot and sit in a comfortable position.
   Bring awareness to each breath. Imagine yourself
   in your mind's eye, and focus your attention there.
2. Say these phrases silently with full attention
   towards yourself:

May I be filled with loving-kindness.
May I be well.
May I be peaceful and at ease.
May I be happy.

3. Repeat these phrases a few times. (You may also express your own thoughts and statements if something else feels right.)

4. Begin to send loving kindness to someone you love very much. (Notice how easy or difficult it is to send love and compassion to this person.)

5. Next, to someone you feel neutral about. (Again, notice how easy or difficult this may be.)

6. Now, choose a difficult person to receive this light. (Notice how easy or difficult this may be.)

7. Send loving kindness, compassion and peace, to everyone you have included in this exercise.

8. Extend it to your community, and finally to encompass the whole world and all the beings on the planet. This meditation will soften and open your heart, leaving you more connected to yourself and to the world around you.

All things by immortal power — near or far,
hiddenly — to each other linked are,
That thou canst not stir a flower —
without troubling of a star . . .
—*Francis Thompson*

We are all sparks of the Divine flame.
—*Hildegard of Bingen*

But neither prayer nor meditation will help you much unless you
constantly put what you learn about divine love into human
practice. All the great sages, from Lao Tzu to Buddha to
Confucius to Jesus, have told us that to experience
the love of God we must give our love
to those around us.
—*Andrew Harvey*

Being in service is another great vehicle for connect-
ing to Spirit and our God-like nature. It can take on a
multitude of forms, ranging from the smallest of deeds
like offering a hug to seemingly more dramatic ones,
like joining the Peace Corps. Irrelevant of scope, when
a giving heart is present, there is an act of service
being performed.

Often, what may seem like very little is actually a great
deal. Active listening is a simple, yet powerful way to
be in service. By creating a sacred space for expres-
sion, you are offering your own Spirit as a silent, and
compassionate participant.

It has been documented that an act of kindness raises the serotonin levels (the feel good chemical) in both the receiver and the giver, and further, anyone witnessing the gesture also benefits. Everyone wins!

So feed the stray cat. Give directions to the lost person. Volunteer your time at a local organization. We have all been there—hungry, lost, in need of an extra hand. Putting yourself in the shoes of another is the quickest way to touch the empathy and compassion in yourself, and opens your heart to being in a state of spiritual service.

Offering my gifts in the service of others
I touch the light within myself.

The day is a gift without time
Moment after moment I unwrap her
I move through her in grace,
no more ahead of myself, or behind,
than a tiger, than a sea gull.
Let me remember
I can open tomorrow the same way.
A slow present
lived as free of time
as the life of a tiger, a sea gull.

—*Sue Silvermarie*

81

Rest is not idleness, and to lie sometimes on the grass under
the trees on a summer's day, listening to the murmur of the
water, or watching the clouds that float across the sky,
is by no means a waste of time.
—*John Lubbock*

Why is it that we find slowing down so difficult? We live in a society whose primary message is: If we are not busy doing something, then we must be wasting time, and surely if we are wasting time, then we must not have any worth. Yet how much real happiness can this endless activity bring?

Our minds, bodies and souls need time to refresh. Being still not only helps to put balance back into our hectic lives, but also creates a space for us to connect with Spirit.

Enjoying nature is a delicious way to abate time and soothe our weary bodies. There's no need to travel very far to experience it, for it is, in fact, all around. We just need to decelerate long enough from our

overbooked lives to admire an oak tree's majesty, relish a sunset's blaze, or smell the lilac's seductive scent of bliss.

Can you recall how healing a day at the beach can feel? Tasting the salty air. Feeling the toasty rays. Hearing the rolling waves. Have you ever considered that the balmy breezes were actually God's breath whispering in your ear? Moving through your senses, could these delicate wafts be the gentle voice of God's guidance and wisdom?

Such simple experiences can leave one feeling balanced, serene, and more connected to the world around you. Continue to discover ways to re-align yourself, with your Self. You will begin to see your life as a sacred journey.

E mpty your mind of all thoughts. Let your heart be at peace . . .
Each separate being in the universe returns to the common
source. Returning to the source is serenity.
— *Tao Te Ching*

Sometimes the best prayer you can make is
just to think that God reads your heart.
—Daniel Considine

For my part, I know nothing with any certainty,
but the sight of stars make me dream.
—Vincent van Gogh

If the sight of the blue skies fills you with joy, if a blade of grass
springing up in the fields has power to move you, if the simple
things of nature have a message that you understand,
rejoice, for your soul is alive.
—*Eleonora Duse*

What is it about the sky that evokes our Spirit? Perhaps her timeless beauty, and expansive presence elicit those same qualities in us. We gaze in awe and wonder, "Is this where my soul began its journey?" "Have my loved ones crossed over to this magnificence?" "Are they looking down and watching us right now?" Though we no longer experience their physical nature, the brilliant, ebony sky reminds us that we are all part of a grand universe, that fills us with hope, eternity, and peaceful reflection.

Remember, we are made of the same particles as stardust! We experience a magical resonance when we gaze up at those heavenly bodies. Engulfed by such beauty and wonder, how can we not sense the spiritual essence that is infused all around us?

Surrounded by natures beauty, I feel Spirits expansive
essence. This timeless quality is also in me,
and I flow into everything possible.

Dreams and Desires

Striving towards your deepest aspirations —manifesting and creating abundance.

The greatest achievement was at first and for a time a dream.
The oak sleeps in the acorn; the bird sleeps in the egg; and in
the highest vision of the soul, a waking angel stirs.
Dreams are the seedlings of realities...
—*James Allen*

Follow your desire as long as you live;
do not lessen the time of following desire, for the
wasting of time is an abomination to the spirit.
—*Ptahhotep 2350 B.C.*

Reach high, for stars lie hidden in your soul.
Dream deep, for every dream precedes the goal.
—*Ralph Vaull Starr*

Listening to your heart is not always simple. Finding out
who you are is not simple. It takes a lot of hard work and
courage to get to know who you are and what you want.
—*George MacDonald*

May you find the path which will lead you to the
highest and truest of yourself.
—*Renée Locks*

Hopes, dreams, and desires are blueprints of the soul.
Like a roadmap, they offer direction and guidance.
Vying for our attention, they make themselves known
by stimulating our emotions, and giving rise to our
creative passions.

Realization of our dreams fills us with a deep sense
of contentment and gratitude. Simply stated—they
make life worth living! Joseph Campbell encourages
us to follow our bliss by utilizing a timeless formula for
spiritual satisfaction—*when you choose the road that brings
you joy, you simultaneously serve the world and yourself.* Life
begins to take on a synchronistic rhythm, and offers
a clear sense of purpose, when you simply align with
what makes you happy.

There's a "voice" inside that calls to you. And like a puppy scratching at the door, it will never be silenced until you offer attention and love. Listen now, or always wonder what could have been.

Take time, get quiet, and listen. What does the mysterious call from within say? How has it shaped your hopes, dreams, and desires? Can you make the choice to follow its prompting now?

When we learn to listen to our inner guidance, and give breath to our deepest longings, we find they are simply urging us to *be more.* More of who we were always meant to be.

> Twenty years from now you will be more disappointed by the things you didn't do than by the ones you did.
> —*Mark Twain*

Start by doing what's necessary, then do
what's possible, and suddenly you are
doing the impossible.
—*St. Francis of Assisi*

Many things which cannot be overcome when
they are together, yield themselves up
when taken little by little.
—*Plutarch*

The creation of a thousand
forests is in one acorn.
—*Ralph Waldo Emerson*

Make visible what, without you,
might never have been seen.
—*Robert Bresson*

Let's face it. It's absolutely fun to daydream! We are effortlessly transported, lost in the realm of our own fantasies, and faraway places where anything's possible. These delightful musings offer clues into our deepest longings, while at the same time, offer space to explore their manifestation. Daydreaming is the mind's way of creatively reflecting back to you your vision.

No dream is impossible. Yet too often we are tempted to give up before we even begin. The mind weighs the long road ahead as too challenging, and makes a formidable case for not yielding to the heart's true longing. "There's not enough time." "It's too difficult." "I'm not good enough." Sound familiar?

Fortunately, the call from within will continue to make itself known until it is fully explored. Regardless of

how overwhelming the task may seem, there's only one thing to do—start from wherever you are. Whether it's changing a career, completing a novel, or reconciling with a loved one…simply begin. Even one small step brings you that much closer to fulfilling your desire.

We all have the capacity to fulfill our desires. Just as a seed holds the potential to bear fruit, so do our daydreams hold the promise to blossom into reality. Plant them in fertile soil, and tend to them often. Let the roots ground, and watch as your cherished dreams flourish. You have just cultivated your own piece of heaven on earth!

Only when we are no longer afraid do we begin to live.
—Anonymous

Though we travel the world over to find the beautiful,
we must carry it with us or we find it not.
—*Ralph Waldo Emerson*

We have forgotten the age-old fact that God speaks
chiefly through dreams and visions.
—*Carl Jung*

Judge of your natural character by what
you do in your dreams.
—*Ralph Waldo Emerson*

Nocturnal dreams are yet another useful resource for excavating our desires. They offer a channel for the subconscious mind to reveal information. Like pieces of a puzzle, dreams come in many shapes. Some don't require analysis because their meaning is fairly obvious, while others choose to present themselves cloaked in mysterious symbols, best left for the dreamer to explore.

Feelings pushed aside during our waking life refuse to be suppressed during sleeping hours. Dreams send key messages informing us of these repressed feelings, whether they're our deepest longings, or worst fears. They play out our day-to-day lives, as if they were homespun movies. By engaging in the interpretation

of our dreams, we gain extraordinary insight into what can no longer remain hidden from consciousness, and at the same time, have a wonderful time dissecting and decoding their illusive meaning.

Our truest life is when we are in dreams awake.
— *Thoreau*

I listen to messages revealed to me through my dreams. I am in the process of aligning with my purpose.

Your vision will become clear only when
you can look into your own heart.
—*Carl Jung*

Throw your heart out — out in front of you
— and run ahead to catch it.
—*Arab proverb*

We all have an idea of the life we'd love to experience. So how do we go about creating it? Start by asking, "What lifts my energy?" "When do I feel most alive?" "What makes me truly happy?" Tell yourself the absolute truth. Do not edit your answers. Remember, it's your vision, and not someone else's image of you.

If answers don't come right away, try meditating. Experience a few moments of stillness. Allow all emotions, sensations, and mental images to surface, for they will offer important clues to accessing your heart's desire.

You can also try visualizing your perfect day, and writing down what you see. Don't leave out any details. Include smells, colors, sounds, locations, and people. Write freely without judgment, and see what image or theme is revealed to you.

Some may enjoy creating a vision collage. Browse through magazines and newspapers, noticing the pictures and words that call to you. Cut out images that represent your desires, and paste them to a poster board. Not only does this exercise help you access your deepest longing, but it also creates a tangible reminder of your vision, which you can reference again and again, keeping you on track to its manifestation.

It's not always easy to see our true vision. But if we allow our hearts to navigate, and pay keen attention to what brings us joy, then, what we most desire, will be revealed.

A man does not learn to understand
anything unless he loves it.

—*Goethe*

Pay attention to what is beginning to awake within you.
The caterpillar can feel the essence of the butterfly
even before it begins to emerge.

—*Dorian Bietz*

Come to the edge, he said. They said: We are afraid.
Come to the edge, he said. They came.
He pushed them . . . and they flew.

—*Guillaume Apollinaire*

When the soul wishes to experience something she
throws an image of the experience out before her
and enters into her own image.

—*Meister Eckhart*

God does not put a longing in our hearts in vain.
—*Saint Therese of Liseux*

A significant aspect to manifesting a dream is believing with your body, mind, and soul that it's truly possible. The universal Law of Attraction states: like attracts like, magnetizing and drawing to us whatever receives our greatest attention.

When we focus mental energy through our thoughts and beliefs, we alter the vibration of our own being. Positive thoughts filled with joy, hope, and peace raise our energetic vibration; negative ones, riddled with doubt, fear, and worry diminish it.

We've all experienced the snowball effect of negativity, right? You're in a bad mood because you inadvertently forgot to pay your credit card bill, and now you owe even more money. This sets off a chain of irritable thoughts that you then put out into the world. It's no surprise when that same, harsh energy comes slamming back at you.

Override oppressive energy by engaging in activities that raise your spirit. Go for a walk, take a bubble bath, or reach out to a friend who can help shift your mindset. If you are so incredibly stuck that you can't even move or speak, then take a deep breath, and silently acknowledge that you're in a deep, defensive reaction. You may not shift right away, but by recognizing your mindset, you are moving in the right direction.

How can we use the law of attraction to create a desired outcome? Begin by simply believing and acting as if it already exists. This will elicit a feeling of accomplishment, thereby raising your energetic vibration. Focusing positive thoughts on your goals is like steadily pulling on a string with your desired outcome at its end. Establish a belief that your desire deserves to be manifested. Remember, you wouldn't have this deep longing in your heart, if your soul didn't seek to express it.

I am a powerfully creative being, and all that I desire is manifesting for my highest good.

When I dare to be powerful — to use my strength
in the service of my vision, then it becomes less
and less important whether I am afraid.

—*Audre Lorde*

Good things happen when we go for it.

—*Alan Webb*

All growth is a leap in the dark. Spontaneous
and without prior experience.

—*Henry Miller*

Faith is the power to stand up to the madness and chaos
of the physical world while holding the position that
nothing external has any authority over what
heaven has in mind for you.

—*Caroline Myss*

Often, we hold a cherished dream, or desire with hope and promise. But doubt and fear will inevitably surface. How can they not? For as much as we yearn for something new to flourish, stepping into unknown territory can simultaneously be unnerving, even terrifying.

If we accept that a certain degree of resistance is a natural part of the growth process, then its ability to have power over us subsides. Fear may be present alongside courage and determination, but it does not have to be in charge.

Leaping into the abyss can be frightening, yet exhilarating! Remain open, even if at first the familiar routine is rattled. With trust and faith present on the journey, the quest for change may lead to extraordinary, and often unexpected places.

If things do not happen as you want them to happen, know that a better way is being found. Trust and never forget that the true way is the way of love. Flowers do not force their way with great strife.

Flowers open to perfection slowly in the Spring.

— *White Eagle*

Self Love

Self-care, self-worth,
self-acceptance — honoring
all that we are, and all that
we can become.

Our deepest fear is not that we are inadequate.
Our deepest fear is that we are powerful beyond
measure. It is our light, not our darkness that most
frightens us. We ask ourselves, who am I to be
brilliant, gorgeous, talented and fabulous? Actually,
who are you not to be? You are a child of God.
Your playing small doesn't serve the world. There is
nothing enlightened about shrinking so that other
people won't feel insecure around you. We were
born to make manifest the glory of God that is
within us. It is not just in some of us: It's in every-
one. And when we let our own light shine, we
unconsciously give other people permission to do
the same. As we are liberated from our own fear,
our presence automatically liberates others.

—*Marianne Williamson*

Awake, my dear
Be kind to your sleeping heart
Take it out into the vast fields of light
And let it breathe
—Hafiz

. . . and then the day came when the risk to
remain tight in a bud was more painful
than the risk it took to blossom.
—Anais Nin

The finest qualities of our nature, like the bloom on
fruits, can be preserved only by the most delicate
handling. Yet we do not treat ourselves
nor one another as tenderly.
—*Henry David Thoreau*

I am with you.
I am here for you.
I will protect you.
I will take care of you.
I will never leave you.
I will honor your feelings.
I will always love you.
I will never betray you.
I accept you exactly as you are.

How many of us long to hear those comforting words
from another? It's safe to venture—EVERYONE.
These simple sentiments echo our profound desire
to be held in the strong arms of unconditional love.
We yearn for another to bestow these compassionate
phrases, yet we wouldn't dream of ever speaking this
way to ourselves. Being our own guardian, caretaker
or best friend.

Considering ourselves first, (not in a selfish or insensitive way), but in a deeply honorable and respectful way, places us on the path to Self Love. By learning to fulfill our own needs, rather than looking to someone or something else to do so, we become stronger and more reliant. Love takes on a fresh, new expression, as we become both giver and receiver. This infusion of "good will towards self" can't help but radiate outward. Acting like a magnet, it will draw others to us, and ironically bring in the external love we long for.

Now, place your hands on your heart, and re-read the opening, self-loving expressions. Allow their comforting energy to melt into your being. Observe what sensations or images arise.

If you feel overwhelmed by life's challenges, or neglect to hold yourself with compassion, try reciting these lines as a form of prayer or meditation.

Wouldn't it be powerful if you fell in love with yourself so deeply that you would do just about anything if you knew it would make you happy? This is precisely how much life loves you and wants you to nurture yourself. The deeper you love yourself, the more the universe will affirm your worth. Then you can enjoy a lifelong love affair that brings you the richest fulfillment from inside out.

—*Alan Cohen*

Self-love can be defined as fully accepting yourself, no matter who or where you are in life. It's bestowing the gifts of kindness, compassion and nurturance to your own being. Simply put, self-love means being good to *YOUR SELF.*

Whether you're a partner, parent or businessperson carrying a mile-long "to do list," (with your needs at the very bottom), or a single person in search of a loving relationship, (who feels like their life won't be complete until that person enters your life), until you learn to give to yourself, your life will pretty much stay the same.

Fulfilling your own needs, even in small ways, will help you to feel nourished, balanced, and more equipped to share your energy and love with others.

Giving to *you* is a way of deeply honoring and loving yourself. Not in extravagant, material ways, but in small, simple practices that can comfort and uplift the spirit.

Here are a few suggestions for pampering and nourishing your senses.

♥ Treat yourself to your favorite bouquet of fresh flowers. Indulge in their sweet fragrance and behold their vibrant colors.

♥ Explore a class you've always been curious about. Try your hand at: digital photography, French cooking, or learning Italian.

♥ Calm the senses with a nature hike, and feel the grounding effect it has on your body and spirit.

♥ Indulge yourself with a beautiful dress, the one that makes you feel like a million bucks!

♥ Relish the peace and quiet of your own company. Solitude is underrated.

♥ Listen to the songbirds in your backyard. Nature's music is melodic and free!

♥ Enjoy a delicious meal at that new restaurant you've been longing to try, alone or with a good friend.

♥ Infuse your surroundings with beauty. Purchase fabrics for your home that express your individual style. Your home is your sanctuary, and should be a source of comfort and joy.

♥ Feel the benefits of a healing massage. Relax and let go of all your worries and stress.

Contributing to the fulfillment of our own needs makes us less needy and demanding of others. By creating loving feelings within, and around us, we naturally attract more love into our lives, while at the same time, holding ourselves in a healthy and comforting space.

Somewhere along our journey of awakening, with all its
struggles, joys, and disappointments, ecstasy will be revealed,
as a confirmation, a blessing, a message from the Source.
Then all that remains is to live with joy, love, and laughter.
—*Margot Anand*

Could a greater miracle take place than for us to
look through each other's eye for an instant?
—*Henry David Thoreau*

There is nothing so healing in all the world
as real presence. Our real presence can
feed the ache for God in others.
—*MacRina Wiederkehr*

According to the Buddha, you can search throughout the entire
universe for someone who is more deserving of your love and
affection than you are yourself, and that person is not to be
found anywhere. You yourself, as much as anybody in
the entire universe, deserve your love and affection.

—*Sharon Salzberg*

Many of us have been taught that it is shameful, or egotistical to let our true power emerge. We shrink behind an invisible, self-imposed curtain designed to obscure our talent and potential, believing that if we "play it safe," we won't lose our friends, family and life, as we know it.

But concealing our grandeur serves no one. In fact it is detrimental to our well-being. We become morose, resentful, even depressed. All the while, yearning to let our inner spark be luminous.

By permitting ourselves to be powerful, we raise our energetic vibration. Others view us as a living example of hope, possibility, and happiness, and feel inspired to join that uplifted state. It is, in a sense, our human responsibility to be all that we can be, and more! Not only to heal ourselves, but to touch all those around us.

I wish I could show you,
When you are lonely or in darkness,
The astonishing light of your own being.
—*Hafiz*

Find the love you seek, by first finding the love within
yourself. Learn to rest in that place within you
that is your true home.
—*Sri Sri Ravi Shankar*

When we do the best we can, we never know what miracle
is wrought in our life or in the life of another.

—*Helen Keller*

We are all teachers, and what we teach is what we need to
learn, and so we teach it over and over again until we learn it.

—A principle of *A Course in Miracles*

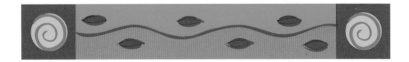

133

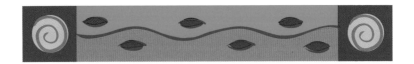

Too often we underestimate the power of a touch, a smile,
a kind word, a listening ear, an honest compliment,
or the smallest act of caring, all of which have the
potential to turn a life around.
—*Leo Buscaglia*

Recall how the simplest gesture of kindness from a stranger left a deep impression in your psyche. How their compassion may have unknowingly helped to give you strength and encouragement, perhaps even changing the course of your life forever. We may never even see that person again, but their presence will never be forgotten.

Trust that you too have wonderful qualities to offer another, which may have more influence than you will ever know. Perhaps it is simply offering consolation to a child who is feeling discouraged, or supporting a friend's dream when they are questioning giving up, or helping that stranger who is lost or hungry.

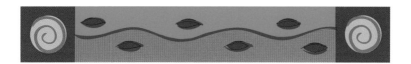

We never really know the full impact a caring act may have on the life of another human being. In fact, it is not for us to know the events that may transpire from our "random act of kindness." Never underestimate yourself, and what you have to offer, for no matter how seemingly small the gesture, the Universe has a grand plan to unfold, and your selfless act of love could be the very catalyst.

> The little unremembered acts of kindness and love are
> the best parts of a person's life.
> — *William Wordsworth*

I know my own true worth and value.
I honor my insight and intuition,
never knowing when it may be
of service to another.

There is a vitality, a life force, an energy, a quickening that is translated through you into action, and because there is only one of you in all of time, this expression is unique. And if you block it, it will never exist through any other medium and it will be lost. The world will not have it. It is not your business to determine how good it is nor how valuable nor how it compares with other expressions. It is your business to keep it yours clearly and directly, to keep the channel open.

—*Martha Graham*

You have your brush, your have your colors,
you paint paradise then in you go.
—*Anatole France*

Creativity is a glorious expression of who we truly are, and absolutely vital to our well-being. Without it, we would lead a spiritless existence.

It connects us to our innate desire to explore our unique gifts—for *no one* will create in the same way that you do. When you suppress the distinctive way you sing, write, cook, dance, garden, sew, or paint, (to name a mere few!), you are depriving both yourself, and the world of the opportunity to feel, grow, and delight in your spirit-fused beauty.

So begin today. Set an intention to express your creativity, no matter how it yearns to unfold. Time, energy, and the desire to let it flow are the basic requirements. Make it a part of your daily routine, like brushing your teeth, or taking a shower. By doing so, you ground

your creative expression into reality, and at the same time, rekindle your deep commitment to practicing self-love. Letting your creativity thrive and shine is a gracious act of compassion you give to yourself.

Imagination will often carry us to worlds that never were. But without it we go nowhere.

—*Carl Sagan*

The only true joy on earth is to escape from the prison of our own false self, and enter by love into union with the Life Who dwells and sings within the essence of every creature and in the core of our own souls.

— *Thomas Merton*

Celebrate your humanness. Celebrate your craziness.
Celebrate your inadequacies. Celebrate your
loneliness. But celebrate you.

—*Leo Buscaglia*

The false self is the part of us that betrays who we really are—our eternal essence. It craves perfection. It casts judgment. It forsakes our true desire in favor of a "safer, more acceptable" choice.

Freedom from these self-imposed chains occurs when we realize we're the ones who created them, and we're the ones who can unlock them. Thomas Merton states, "The only way to true freedom is through knowing who we truly are."

Through self-discovery, we come to meet our true Self, that which is both Divine and human. By learning to love and appreciate ourselves, we learn to honor our very core. We become less concerned with external

perfection and approval from others. The false self is no longer running the show. It is from this expanded place that we begin to experience our authentic freedom.

Spirituality is laying claim to your gifts. I want to be that person that I'm capable of being. We think we're not happy because of what we're not getting. But really we're not happy because of what we're not giving.

—*Marianne Williamson*

What you do for yourself— any gesture of kindness, any gesture of gentleness, any gesture of honesty and clear seeing toward yourself— will affect how you experience your world. In fact, it will transform how you experience the world. What you do for yourself, you're doing for others, and what you do for others, you're doing for yourself.

—*Charlotte Kasl*

When we feel love and kindness toward others, it not only makes others feel loved and cared for, but it help us also to develop inner hapiness and peace.

—*His Holiness the Dalai Lama*

Energy is by nature a reciprocal force: what we give out is what we receive. When we are gentle, tender and practice self-love, compassion will be our mirror. If we are harsh, critical and practice self-loathing, the world will reflect those back to us.

The more we can make nurturing ourselves with compassion and love a habit (so much so that they become our default mechanism during challenging times) the more of these heart-centered qualities we can offer to others. By changing your inner view, your outer world automatically changes with you.

Compassion is one of the principal things that make our lives meaningful. It is the source of all lasting happiness and joy. And it is the foundation of a good heart, the heart of one who acts out of a desire to help others. There is no denying that our happiness is inextricably bound up with the happiness of others. There is no denying that if society suffers, we ourselves suffer. Nor is there any denying that the more our hearts and minds are afflicted with ill-will, the more miserable we become. Thus we can reject everything else: religion, ideology, all received wisdom. But we cannot escape the necessity of love and compassion.

—*His Holiness the Dalai Lama*

I no longer try to change outer things. They are simply
a reflection. I change my inner perception and the
outer reveals the beauty so long obscured by my
own attitude. I concentrate on my inner vision
and find my outer view transformed.

—*Daily Word*

Beauty is not a need but an ecstasy. It is not a mouth
thirsting nor an empty hand stretched forth, but rather
a heart enflamed and a soul enchanted.

—*Kahlil Gibran*

Making yourself more beautiful is dependent on giving yourself more love. Loving yourself is deeply nourishing and healing. It satisfies you in ways that no other form of love can. When we love ourselves, a mysterious array of chemicals and emotions align, making us physically and emotionally balanced, even radiant. When we love ourselves on a daily basis, our beauty grows very rapidly.

—*Susan West Kurz*

The definition of beauty is as varied and personal as beauty itself. We live in a society that often puts emphasis on outward, physical beauty, yet we all know that externals do not complete the entire picture. Most of us would never judge a person's sole value by their appearance, yet we don't offer ourselves the same acceptance. We are harsh and critical for not looking a certain way, forgetting all the wonderful attributes that comprise our whole being.

When we value our natural, intrinsic qualities such as empathy in nurturing a broken friend, courage in pursuing a sacred passion, or patience in dealing with a stressful event, the luminous spark of our inner beauty can't help but shine through. If we feel good about who we are and what we offer, that feeling will radiate externally, like the infectious joy in a child's laughter.

Beauty has often been said to be in the eye of the beholder. But it is we who must learn to behold the beauty within ourselves. And when we love and appreciate ourselves, both inside and out, that beauty is deliciously irresistible.

I love and accept myself just as I am.
—Louise Hay

If one advances confidently in the direction of his dreams, and endeavors to live the life which he has imagined, he will meet with a success unexpected in common hours.

—*Henry Thoreau*

I beg you... to have patience with everything unresolved in your heart and try to love the questions themselves as if they were locked rooms or books written in a very foreign language. Don't search for the answers, which could not be given you now, because you would not be able to live them. And the point is, to live everything. Live the questions now. Perhaps then, some-day far in the future, you will gradually, without ever noticing it, live your way into the answer...

—*Rainer Maria Rilke*

153

Even if our efforts of attention seem for years to be
producing no results, one day a light that is in exact
proportion to them will flood the soul.

—*Simon Weil*

Traditional success can be measured by one's achieve-
ments. But true success is a state of mind that is
ascertained by how happy and fulfilled we feel. Have
we lived fully? Loved unconditionally? Followed our
soul's yearning? How much have we allowed our-
selves to enjoy the extraordinary journey of becoming
who we are? The answers to these questions are what
determine a truly, authentic state of success.

By staying on a conscious path, we gain insight as to
what is most important. The soul begins to experi-
ence what is always yearned for, and expresses itself
through *divine qualities* such as the *loving* parent, the
giving volunteer, the *compassionate* friend, the *guiding*
teacher, the *creative* artist, or the *benevolent* employer.

The actual role becomes less important compared to how it is lived.

By listening to the call of your soul, and allowing it to express Divine qualities you will ultimately manifest what once only lived in the realm of your imagination. *This* is authentic success, and self-love.

To have played and laughed with enthusiasm, and sung with exultation, to know even one life has breathed easier because you have lived — this is to have succeeded.
—*Ralph Waldo Emerson*

I listen to the voice within. I follow my bliss.
I am patient with myself, knowing that my dreams
are evolving in a timely manner.

Special Thanks

Many thanks to my friends and family who supported me along this creative journey. It has been an ever-changing process, a metamorphosis of sorts, similar to that of a caterpillar becoming a butterfly. Much gratitude to all of you who have helped give this book its wings.

A special thanks to Rosemary Serluca, a wonderful friend and editor, and whose intuitive sensibilities so lovingly helped to shape this book. Your belief, enthusiasm and encouragement was always felt. Thanks for holding the light.

To my dear friend Julie Moriva—Thank you for believing in the beauty of this project and for your infinitely optimistic spirit and encouraging words.

To Fred Glover, Deni Javas and Leslie Gold for your enduring support and thoughtful insights. And to all who have offered guidance, a kind word, or contribution, your support was deeply felt.

♥Part of the proceeds from this book will be donated to Best Friends Animal Society.

About the Author

Jenny Vainisi is an accomplished designer, award winning illustrator, and arts educator. She has created numerous illustrations for the publishing and advertising markets in her unique, idyllic brand. She is a certified holistic healer and holds a degree in Reiki. She believes that art provides a space for nurturing creative expression, confidence and compassion.

Jenny currently resides in Brooklyn, New York with two furry companions, Ollie and Luca.

For more information, please visit
www.embracingyourlifebook.com
www.jennyvainisi.com

Tell me, what is it you plan to do with your
one wild and precious life?
— *Mary Oliver*

It is up to you to illumine the earth.
—*Philippe Vensier*

What makes your own heart sing, is what you
were placed here on earth to do.
—*unknown*